Sick All the Time
Kids with Chronic Illness

Kids with Special Needs

Sick All the Time
Kids with Chronic Illness

by Zachary Chastain and Camden Flath

MASON CREST PUBLISHERS INC.
370 Reed Road
Broomall, Pennsylvania 19008
(866)MCP-BOOK (toll free)
www.masoncrest.com

First Printing
9 8 7 6 5 4 3 2 1

ISBN (set) 978-1-4222-1727-6   ISBN (pbk set) 978-1-4222-1918-8

Library of Congress Cataloging-in-Publication Data

Chastain, Zachary.
  Sick all the time : kids with chronic illness / by Zachary Chastain and Camden Flath.
      p. cm.
  Includes bibliographical references and index.
  ISBN 978-1-4222-1719-1   ISBN (pbk) 978-1-4222-1922-5
  1. Chronic diseases in children—Juvenile literature. 2. Chronically ill children—Juvenile literature. I. Flath, Camden, 1987– II. Title.
  RJ380.C43 2010
  618.92'044—dc22
                              2010012758

Produced by Harding House Publishing Service, Inc.
www.hardinghousepages.com
Design by MK Bassett-Harvey.
Cover design by Torque Advertising Design.
Printed in the USA by Bang Printing.

Photo Credits
Creative Commons Attribution 2.0 Generic/Unported: Maki, Giovanni: pg. 33, mia3mom: pg 29; GNU Free Documentation License, Version 1.2: Erik1980: pg. 39; morgueFile: jdurham: pg. 41; United States Air Force: Meares, Senior Airman Mike: pg. 42; United States Marine Corps: Biscuiti, Sgt Scott: pg. 38.

The creators of this book have made every effort to provide accurate information, but it should not be used as a substitute for the help and services of trained professionals.

Introduction

To the Teacher

Kids with Special Needs provides a unique forum for demystifying a wide variety of childhood medical and developmental disabilities. Written to captivate an elementary-level audience, the books bring to life the challenges and triumphs experienced by children with common chronic conditions such as hearing loss, intellectual disability, physical differences, and speech difficulties. The topics are addressed frankly through a blend of fiction and fact.

This series is particularly important today as the number of children with special needs is on the rise. Over the last two decades, advances in pediatric medical techniques have allowed children who have chronic illnesses and disabilities to live longer, more functional lives. At the same time, IDEA, a federal law, guarantees their rights to equal educational opportunities. As a result, these children represent an increasingly visible part of North American population in all aspects of daily life. Students are exposed to peers with special needs in their classrooms, through extracurricular activities, and in the community. Often, young people have misperceptions and unanswered questions about a child's disabilities—and more important, his or her abilities. Many times, there is no vehicle for talking about these complex issues in a comfortable manner.

This series will encourage further conversation about these issues. Most important, the series promotes a greater comfort for its readers as they live, play, and study side by side with these children who have medical and developmental differences—kids with special needs.

—*Dr. Carolyn Bridgemohan*
Boston Pediatric Hospital/Harvard Medical School

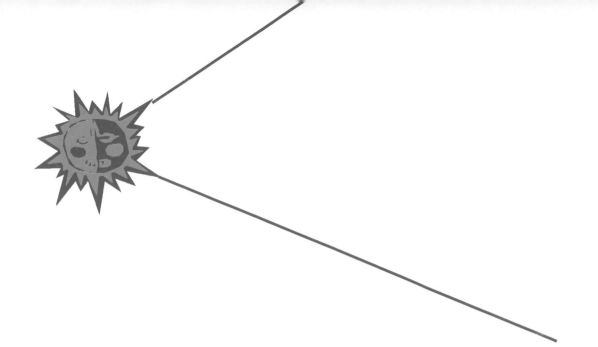

Dylan loves to travel. He still remembers that one of the best days of his life back when he was just a little kid was the day he saw his dad take the car seat out of their car. When his dad came inside, he told Dylan, "From now on, when it's just you and me, you sit in the front seat."

Since then, Dylan has loved to travel. He likes to take trips with just his dad so he can sit up front and tell him where to turn left or right.

On Dylan's last birthday, his dad and mom bought him a huge map of the United States, the country where they live. They pinned it to the kitchen wall and poked tiny flags made of toothpicks into it. They stuck the flags to all the places Dylan had traveled to outside his hometown.

Sometimes when Dylan looks at those tiny flags, he also says to himself, *I had a seizure on that trip. No seizures on that trip or that one or that one. Seizure on that trip, but not on that one. . . .*

Dylan has had epilepsy for as long as he can remember. When he was a baby, his parents thought he might die. But his doctors gave him a medicine that helped control his seizures, and ever since then, he doesn't have as many seizures. When he does, they're small ones. They're not dangerous—but Dylan hates the

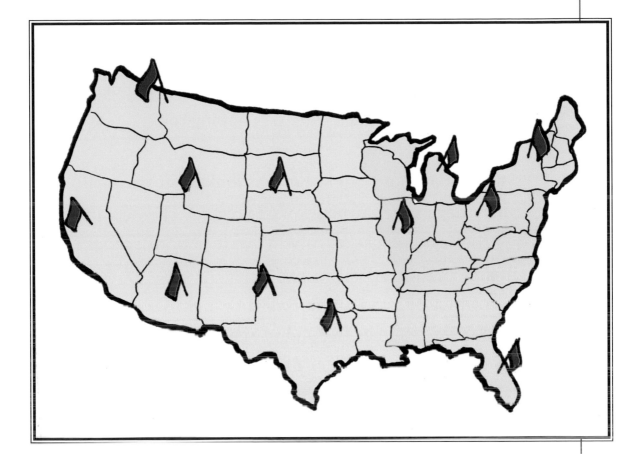

way they feel. And he hates knowing that people are staring at him while he's out of control of his body, wondering why that kid is twitching and jerking like that.

For the past six months, though, Dylan hasn't had a single seizure. He knows his mom and dad are hoping he's finally outgrowing his epilepsy. That happens sometimes. And that's what he's hoping too.

On Monday morning, Dylan was looking at the map full of flags as he slurped down his cereal. He was eating too fast because he couldn't wait to be at school. This week they were learning about the great explorers of history, something Dylan thought was really interesting—and at the end of the week, on Friday, his class was taking a field trip to New York City. Dylan had never been there, and he really wanted to put a flag on his map on the big dot that was labeled "New York City."

He was so excited that he grabbed his backpack and started out the door without taking his medicine.

"Dylan! Wait!" His mom handed him a pill and a big glass of water.

Dylan gulped it down. Then he stared at his mom and let out a huge BURP.

"Disgusting!" His mom was trying to sound angry, but Dylan knew she was laughing. He turned and ran out the door, laughing too.

Every day at school, Dylan spent an hour with Mr. Davies, his resource room teacher. Dylan's epilepsy made it hard for him to learn things as quickly as the other kids at school. Especially math. Mr. Davies spent an hour every day helping Dylan keep up with the rest of the class. It was no big deal, really. Mr. Davies helped two or three other kids in Dylan's class for an hour a day too.

The end of the school day finally arrived, and their teacher turned off the lights to show a video on explorers. Everyone began their about-to-watch-a-movie jobs: Sarah closed the door and pulled down the shades, Jamie turned on the T.V. and the DVD player, and Dylan ran to do his job—erasing the chalkboard. He jumped up and down to erase the words at the very top of the board. He was almost finished when he suddenly stopped, and stood still, staring at the board. *Oh no.* He felt his muscles start to shake, and then he went away. . . .

The next thing he knew, the school nurse was standing over him, saying his name. "Dylan? Dylan, can you hear me?"

Dylan blinked. His head hurt and his neck muscles ached, but he could hear her. "Yes," he whispered.

The nurse smiled down at him. "Don't worry, Dylan, you're going to be okay. I called your mom, and she's on her way here."

Dylan lay still, his eyes shut. He could hear his teacher, Ms. Popple, talking to the nurse. "He was perfectly fine all day," she was saying. "We were about to watch a video and he was cleaning the chalkboard when he just stopped and went into a seizure."

Ms. Popple knew about Dylan's epilepsy. Dylan knew that before the school year started, his parents and the school nurse had explained to Ms. Popple what to do in case Dylan ever had a seizure. But until today he'd never had one in school.

He rolled over on his side and looked at the door, waiting for his mom to walk through it. A lot of things were going to change now, he thought. He rubbed his eyes with his knuckles so his mother wouldn't think he was crying when she got there.

The next day, Dylan and his mom sat in their doctor's waiting room. Dylan kept glancing sideways at his mother. He wouldn't have been all that worried if his mom didn't look so worried. But she did look worried. She was trying to hide it, Dylan knew, because every time she caught his eye, she gave him a fake-looking smile. So he just sat in his chair and waited, and tried to picture what New York City would look like in four days.

Finally Dr. Kelly called them into her office. She did all the usual stuff—"Open your mouth and say ah"—and shone her little light into Dylan's eyes and ears and nose. She asked Dylan about how his body felt and if any part of it hurt, and Dylan said no, he felt fine.

"Well," Dr. Kelly said, "I'm not sure what happened. Let's wait a few more days to see if any more seizures occur. If they do, we'll have you spend a night at the hospital and see what we can find. Sound good?"

No! Dylan thought. It did NOT sound good. He hated being in the hospital, hated the bright lights and the funny smell. But he looked at his mom, and he could see she seemed less worried now, so he nodded his head yes.

"Good," said Doctor Kelly. "I think you're going to be just fine."

By that night, Dylan was starting to worry. Not so much about his epilepsy but about the trip to New

York City on Friday. His parents had been talking in their bedroom with the door closed for almost an hour. What if they decided he couldn't go on the field trip this Friday? Dylan shut his eyes against the idea. He would keep himself from having a seizure before then, he decided. He would just make up his mind not to let one happen. No matter what.

When his mom came into his bedroom to say goodnight, she brought a baby monitor, the kind that lets parents in one room hear the noises their child is making in another room. The monitor let his parents know if he had a seizure in his sleep.

Dylan made a face at it. "Mom, no!"

They hadn't used the monitor for more than a year, not since he'd had seizures more often. Looking at it now just made him feel worse.

"I'm sorry," his mom said, "I know you hate this. I don't like it either. But please do it for me, just for a few nights. Dad and I will sleep better."

Dylan sighed. "Okay. But only for a few nights."

His mom smiled. It was a tired smile, but this one was real. "Your dad's coming in to read you a chapter out of *Vasquez, Famous Explorer*, okay? I love you buddy."

After the story was over and lights were out, Dylan closed his eyes and concentrated on feeling normal, being normal. When he finally fell asleep, he dreamed of hundreds of people on crowded streets and tall buildings that scraped the sky.

As soon as Dylan woke up, he knew he was in the hospital. He could tell by the bright lights and the funny smell.

His mom and dad were sitting close beside the bed. "Hey buddy," his dad said, "how you feeling?"

"What happened?" Dylan whispered.

His mom tried to smile, but he could tell she had been crying. "You had a seizure in your sleep. We heard you on the monitor. It was a bad one this time. We called 911, and the ambulance came."

Dylan swallowed the lump in his throat and tried to pretend he was a grownup. "A tonic-clonic?" he asked, using the word he knew the doctors would use for what his parents called a grand mal seizure.

His dad nodded. "That's right, buddy."

Dylan stared up at the bright white light above his head for a few moments, and then he screwed up his courage to ask, "But I can still go on the fieldtrip to New York City, right? I'll be fine by then."

"We'll see," his mom said. "The neurologist and Dr. Kelly are coming in to talk to us soon. We'll see what they say."

After the doctors left his room, Dylan's dad took off the baseball cap he wore almost all day, every day, and put it on Dylan's head. This was what he did when they were going to have a family meeting. It meant that Dylan was expected to talk with them as though he were an equal, so they could figure out together what to do about something serious.

Dylan pushed himself up against the pillow and squared his shoulders. He was going to do his best not to cry.

Together, he and his parents decided some things were going to have to change. For one thing, Dylan would be taking a new medicine. He would still go to school, but Dr. Kelly said things would be different. He would have to have a "special buddy" with him when his teacher wasn't in the room, and (Dylan really hated this part) he would have to use the bathroom in the nurse's office.

"This is just part of having epilepsy, Dylan," said his dad. "Things change, and we have to change with them."

His mom smiled. "Actually, Dylan, that's just the way life is, whether you have epilepsy or not. You just have to learn to deal with changes and get on with life."

Dylan nodded. His parents were taking him home in the morning, and the only thing he cared about was making it to Friday without having another seizure. He knew that if he could do that, his mom and dad might still let him go to New York City with his class.

You better do your job, he said silently to the new medicine already sitting in a little bottle beside the bed.

It was Thursday before Dylan's parents were ready to let him go back to school. Dylan felt restless and impatient, but at least he hadn't had a seizure. Maybe the new medicine would make things go back to the way they had been before.

His mom and dad drove him to school early that morning, and they went in with him to meet with Ms. Popple, the school psychologist, and the new aide that would be spending his day with Dylan now.

As his parents said goodbye, Dylan's stomach was suddenly full of butterflies. He followed Ms. Popple down the hallway to their classroom, but his feet moved more and more slowly. He didn't want to face the other kids. Were they going to think he was weird now?

Ms. Popple opened the door and stood aside for Dylan to go through. He stepped inside and then came to a stop, his eyes frozen on a giant banner that hung from the ceiling.

"WELCOME BACK, DYLAN!" was written in huge rainbow letters across the banner. He could see that everyone in his class written on their names on it. Someone yelled, "He's here!" and everyone gathered around Dylan. They gave him the get-well-soon cards they had made him while he was away. They had been learning about epilepsy while he was gone, and they were full of questions. Dylan found that talking about epilepsy as though it were something normal made him feel better. All the butterflies in his stomach flew away. He grinned at his friends and told them about the gross food he'd had to eat in the hospital.

As the day went by, though, he noticed that a few kids weren't talking to him anymore. In fact, they barely looked at him. They looked like they were scared of him, he decided.

A couple of kids talked to Dylan too much. They were kids he'd never particularly been friends with before, and now they acted as though they were his best friends. They made him feel weird, like the only thing they liked about him was that he was a sick kid.

But at least no one laughed at him or said anything mean.

That night, as Dylan and his parents were sitting at the table, Dylan smiled as he crunched on a carrot. It had been three days since his big seizure, three days with no more seizures.

"What are you smiling about?" his dad asked.

Dylan swallowed a mouthful of carrot, and then he shouted, "New York City tomorrow!"

"Woah!" his mother said. "Wait a second, I thought we told you—"

Dylan interrupted, "You never said no. You just said we'd wait and see. And we did, and I'm FINE, so can I go? Please, Dad?" Dylan looked at his father. He knew in these situations his dad said yes way more often than his mom.

"Dylan . . . I don't know. . . ." His dad looked worried. "It's only been a few days. We really can't know for sure if the new medicine is working. We don't want you have a seizure so far from home."

Dylan knew he had to think fast, so he stood up from his place at the table, walked over to his dad, and took off his dad's baseball cap. He put the cap on his own head and sat back down. "Family meeting," he announced, "to decide if Dylan goes to New York City tomorrow."

Dylan had never done this. His parents looked at each other. Then they started laughing.

"I guess you're in charge, huh, Dylan?" His dad laughed. "Well, here are my rules. If you're going to New York City tomorrow, I have to go too. We'll drive

down separately in the car, following the bus the whole way. And when we get there, we'll be with your class. The only difference is you'll have to be with your dad all day."

Dylan thought for a moment. If his dad went too, kids might think he was weird. But there were always parents who went along on fieldtrips, so maybe no one would think this was anything all that different. And if Dylan went in his dad's car, he could yell directions at father.

Dylan grinned. He loved yelling directions at his dad. "Deal!" he told his dad.

After all, the important thing was New York City. He couldn't wait to put a new flag on the map.

Kids and Chronic Illness

Kids all over the world have illnesses that cannot be cured. These are called *chronic* illnesses. Unlike a broken bone that will heal with time or a cold that fades after a few days, a chronic illness can affect a child for her entire life. Kids who have some type of chronic illness may need to take medicine for a long time. Some chronic illnesses will require that kids make changes in their everyday lives. Different types of chronic illness can change the way a kid eats, breathes, moves, or acts.

Though chronic illness can have a big impact on a kid's life, a child with chronic illness is much more than his medical condition. Kids with chronic illness aren't all that different from kids who don't have a chronic illness. They can be great students, friends, athletes, and artists. Kids who have a chronic illness simply have another *challenge* to face that other kids don't.

Chronic means that something is permanent or recurs often.

A challenge is something hard that must be faced and overcome.

What Is a Chronic Illness?

A chronic illness is a sickness that lasts for a long time or comes back again and again. Doctors may be able to treat the symptoms of a chronic illness but not cure it. A kid who has a chronic illness may have had that illness since she was born. Some kids may develop a chronic illness later in life.

Many different types of diseases and conditions can be called chronic illnesses. Some of these conditions are serious and some are milder. For instance, *allergies* are one form of chronic illness. Kids who have allergies may have those allergies for the rest of their lives. They may take medicine to keep their eyes from watering or nose from running, but they will still have allergies. Some allergies aren't all that serious, but others can be very dangerous. For instance, some kids who are allergic to peanuts, might go into shock and even die if they eat foods that contain peanuts. Avoiding peanuts can change the way a child lives his life. Other types of chronic illness can change a

> *Allergies are when someone is unusually sensitive to something such as dust, pollen, animals, or foods. Allergies can make you sneeze. They can give you itchy rashes or make you sick to your stomach.*

These peanut butter brownies look delicious, but could be deadly to a child with a peanut allergy. Choosing only foods that promise to be peanut free is the safest option for a child with a peanut allergy.

child's life even more. A child with diabetes, for example, will have to make changes to the way that she eats. She may have to have shots every day.

While some chronic illnesses are rare, many are very common. Asthma, a chronic illness that causes trouble breathing, is quite common among children.

Types of Chronic Illness

Each kind of chronic illness has its own set of *symptoms*. Often, these symptoms are completely different from one illness to another. The only thing that these illnesses have in common is that they don't go away.

Here are a few examples of chronic illness.

Asthma

Asthma is a chronic illness that affects the airways in the lungs. Kids with asthma may have trouble breathing. They may wheeze, cough a lot, or have chest pain. The symptoms of asthma can get worse when they run or exercise.

Diabetes

Diabetes is a chronic illness that prevents the body from making or using a chemical called insulin. Insulin helps the body turn the food you eat into the energy you need. Without enough insulin, the body cannot take in energy from food properly, causing sugar to build up in the blood. When this happens, it's called high blood sugar. It can cause many different health problems.

Symptoms are the signs that tell doctors you have a disease or health condition. The same symptom can sometimes be a sign for more than one illness or disorder. For instance, a runny nose can be a symptom that you have a cold—or it could be a symptom that you're allergic to something in the air.

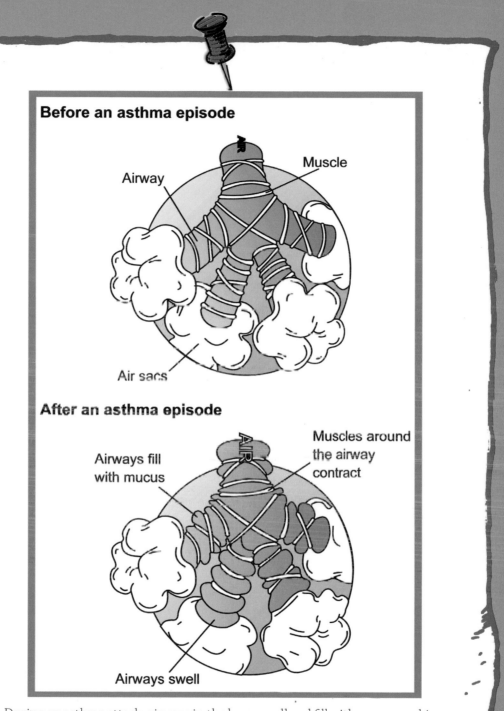

Before an asthma episode

Airway

Muscle

Air sacs

After an asthma episode

Airways fill
with mucus

Muscles around
the airway
contract

Airways swell

During an asthma attack, airways in the lungs swell and fill with mucus, making breathing more difficult.

There are two main types of diabetes. Type 1 diabetes keeps the body from making insulin. It often begins when people are still children. Type 2 diabetes keeps the body from using insulin the way it is supposed to. It usually doesn't start until a person is older.

Epilepsy

Epilepsy is a disorder that causes people to have seizures. A seizure happens when a person's brain sends out an electrical signal too strong for the body to handle. A per-

PANCREAS

INSULIN

BLOOD SUGAR

The pancreas normally produces insulin, which allows the body to turn sugar into energy, thereby lowering blood sugar levels. Diabetes occurs when the body does not make insulin and sugar collects in the blood.

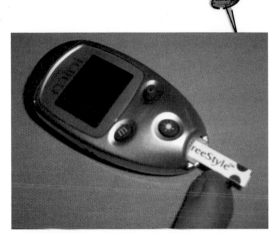

A child with diabetes will have to learn how to test his blood sugar levels regularly.

son who does not have epilepsy can have a seizure because of drug use or a head injury. If someone has many seizures that aren't caused by these things, however, a doctor may **diagnose** him as having epilepsy.

Lupus

Lupus is a type of illness called an autoimmune disease. An autoimmune disease causes a person's **immune system** to attack the body it is meant to protect. Lupus can cause pain in the joints, long-lasting fever, and rashes on the skin. More serious forms of lupus cause the immune system to harm important organs, such as the kidneys.

*To **diagnose** means to figure out what is wrong with someone. It's what doctors do when they decide what sickness or condition you have.*

*Your **immune system** is the parts of your body that fight off germs and other invaders. Your immune system is meant to keep you from getting sick.*

Sickle Cell Anemia

Sickle cell anemia is a disease passed down through families in which red blood cells form an abnormal crescent shape. (Red blood cells are normally shaped like a disc.) Symptoms usually don't occur until after a child is four months old, but then they can last a lifetime. Almost all patients with sickle cell anemia have painful episodes (crises), which can last from hours to days. These crises can affect the bones of the back, the long bones, and the chest. Some children have one episode every few years. Others have many episodes per year. The crises can be severe enough to require a hospital stay.

Fatigue is another word for extreme tiredness.

A syndrome is a group of symptoms that together indicate a medical condition.

Other Types of Chronic Illness

- Skin conditions such as eczema (which causes skin to become dry and itchy) and some cases of acne.
- Heart disease, a condition that causes the heart to not work properly, leading to heart attacks.
- Chronic *fatigue syndrome*, which causes a person to be overly tired more often than usual.

What Causes Chronic Illness?

The causes of chronic illness are often as different as the illnesses themselves. Chronic illnesses can be caused by many different things. Rather than having just one cause, many doctors and scientists believe that most chronic illnesses are caused by a combination of things.

Some chronic illnesses are genetic. This means these illnesses can be passed from parent to child, from generation to generation.

Though our *genes* do shape our health, children whose parents never had a chronic

Genes are the material inside your cells that create the map for what you look like, how smart you are, and some of the illnesses or other conditions you might have. Your genes come to you from your parents.

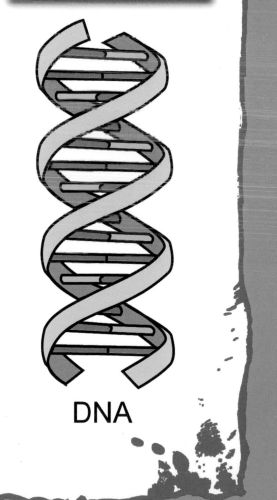

DNA

All our genetic information is stored in something called DNA. The pieces that make up DNA form a code that helps make us who we are.

illness may develop a chronic illness. In the same way, while the genes we get from our parents may make it more likely that we get a chronic illness or disease, they don't always mean we will definitely get a certain illness. Whether someone has a chronic illness doesn't always depend only on their genes.

Chronic illnesses can also be caused by a person being around something in the environment. Certain foods, chemicals, or poisons can cause a person to develop a chronic illness. Even *stress* can lead to some chronic illnesses. Many doctors believe that a mix of both genetic and things in the environment cause chronic illness.

> *Stress is your body's reaction to anything that means you have to change or adjust yourself, mentally, physically, or emotionally.*

Diagnosing Chronic Illnesses

Diagnosing chronic illnesses can be hard to do. Doctors and parents may even think that a kid is imagining his symptoms, making it harder to get a diagnosis. Children who have always felt sick may even think their pain or symptoms are normal, so they may not mention their symptoms to their parents. As a result, sometimes chronic illness may not be diagnosed for a long time.

Once parents and doctors think that they know what symptoms a child is showing, a diagnosis can still be difficult to get. Many chronic illnesses share symptoms. Problems like soreness or tiredness can point to more than one type of chronic illness. This makes it even harder for doctors to get a correct diagnosis. In some cases, different doctors may give different diagnoses based on the same symptoms. As a result, families may feel confused—and children may not get the treatment they need as quickly as they might have otherwise.

Before getting a diagnosis, many kids may feel like no one knows how they are feeling. They may feel like others don't believe them when they say they are in pain. It can be scary not to understand why you feel the way you do. Once a child has a diagnosis, she can also begin getting the treatment she needs. This will also mean she can start to feel better.

How Are Chronic Illnesses Treated?

Different chronic illnesses are treated differently. Here are a few examples of treatments for different chronic illnesses.

Asthma

Asthma is treated in two ways. First, kids with asthma will take medicine that stops them from having an asthma attack where they can't breathe easily. Second, kids must take medicine during an asthma attack to keep it from getting worse. Kids with asthma often use an inhaler to take their medicine by breathing it in. It's also important for kids with asthma to avoid the things that cause them to have an asthma attack (such as very cold air, smoke, or dust).

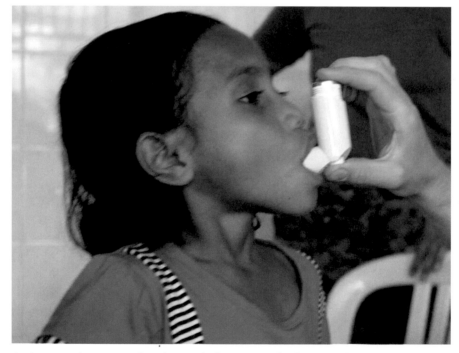

Asthma is often treated with an inhaler. This girl is learning how to use her new inhaler.

Epilepsy

Epilepsy symptoms can be controlled, but the illness cannot be cured. Kids who have epilepsy take medicine to control their seizures. If a child who has epilepsy takes her medicine, she will not have as many seizures, or she may have no seizures at all. If the child stops taking her medicine, she will have seizures again. Some people may grow out of epilepsy, but many people have epilepsy for their entire lives.

Lupus

Lupus can be treated with medication. People who have mild forms of lupus can treat their illness by taking medicines like Advil® and aspirin (though children should not take aspirin). More serious types of lupus may require stronger medicines.

Sickle Cell Anemia

Children with sickle cell disease need ongoing treatment, even when they are not having a painful crisis. They should take folic acid (to help make red blood cells). During painful episodes, they will need to use pain medicines and drink plenty of fluids.

Chronic Illness and Special Education

For many kids with some type of chronic illness, *special education* will be the best way for them to succeed in school. Special education can help kids with chronic illness work around their illness.

A kid with a chronic illness may miss a lot of school because of his sickness. Students who miss classes or some assignments because of doctor visits, for example, can get a special teacher to help them make up what they missed. Kids might also need special *therapy* at school to help them with the effects of chronic illness. Physical therapy, for instance, helps kids with movements like walking, sitting, or standing. Kids with chronic illness may also need to leave class to take medicine during the school day. Some kids may have problems learning because their illnesses change the way their brains work. Special education teachers or aides can help them succeed

Special education teaches kids who have trouble learning because of some disability.

Therapy is any kind of treatment that's meant to help an illness or injury get better.

A child with a chronic illness might have trouble learning, or may have to miss a
lot of school for doctor appointments.

in school. These kinds of special changes in the school day and others can help kids with chronic illness.

A law called the Individuals with Disabilities Education Act (IDEA) outlines how schools should decide which kids need special education. In order to *qualify* for special education under IDEA, the child's chronic illness must get in the way of her learning new material, understanding schoolwork, or taking part in school activities. The IDEA law lists thirteen different kinds of disabilities that may

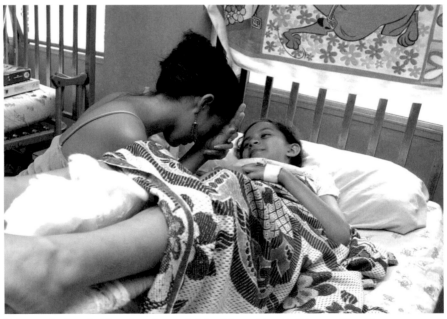

Life might be challenging for a child with a chronic illness. Her illness, as well as daily doses of medicine and frequent doctor and hospital visits might make her feel different from other children. Support, love and respect from family and friends will help her lead a happy life.

mean a child will qualify for special education. Chronic illness is covered under the "other health impairment" *category* under the law.

The IDEA law requires that:

- the child has problems performing well at school activities.
- the child's parent, teacher, or other school staff person must ask that the child be examined for a disability.
- the child is *evaluated* to decide if she does indeed have a disability and to figure out what kind of special education she needs.
- a group of people, including the kid's parents, teachers, and the *school psychologist*, meets to decide on a plan for helping him. This plan is called an Individualized Education

To *qualify* means to fit the definition of something or to meet the requirements.

A *category* is a group or a certain kind of thing.

When something is *evaluated*, it is examined to see in which category it belongs.

A *school psychologist*'s job in the school is to help evaluate kids who are having a hard time learning, for whatever reason and set up educational plans for them. She may give tests to kids, spend time talking with them about their feelings and problems, and work with teachers to make sure that all kids with special needs are getting the education they need to do well.

Program (IEP). The IEP spells out exactly what the child needs in order to succeed at school.

Succeeding With Chronic Illness

A chronic illness can be a tough thing for a kid to deal with. It might mean that they need see doctors quite often, more than kids who don't have a chronic illness. Children with chronic illness might need to take medicine for their illness for a very long time, possibly the rest of their lives. They may not be able to eat the same things other kids do, or they may not be able to do the things other kids their age can do.

Though they may face challenges, children with chronic illness can learn to cope with their illness and find ways to do many of the things they enjoy. And like all of us, kids with chronic illness do better when they know they are respected and accepted.

Further Reading

Abramovitz, M. *Lupus*. San Diego, Calif.: Lucent Books, 2007.

Abramovitz, M. *Muscular Dystrophy*. San Diego, Calif.: Lucent Books, 2007.

Abrams, L. *Diseases and Disorders—Chronic Fatigue Syndrome*. San Diego, Calif.: Lucent Books, 2003.

Bender, L. *Explaining Epilepsy*. North Mankato, Minn.: Smart Apple Media, 2009.

Bjorklund, R. *Epilepsy*. New York: Benchmark Books, 2006.

Brill, M. T. *Multiple Sclerosis*. New York: Benchmark Books, 2007.

Gray, S. W. *Living With Asthma*. Mankato, Minn.: Child's World, 2002.

Haugen, H. M. *Understanding Diseases and Disorders—Epilepsy*. Farmington Hills, Mich.: KidHaven Press, 2004.

Johnson, P. *Muscular Dystrophy*. New York: Rosen Publishing, 2008.

Peacock, J. *Diabetes*. Mankato, Minn.: Capstone Press, 2000.

Royston, A. *Explaining Asthma*. North Mankato, Minn.: Smart Apple Media, 2009.

Semple, C. M. *Diabetes*. Berkeley Heights, N.J.: Enslow Publishers, 2000.

Find Out More on the Internet

American Sickle Cell Anemia Association
www.ascaa

American Chronic Pain Association
www.theacpa.org

American Diabetes Association
www.diabetes.org

American Lyme Disease Foundation
www.aldf.com

The CFIDS Association of America (Chronic Fatigue Syndrome)
www.cfids.org

Chronic-Illness.org
www.chronic-illness.org

Epilepsy Foundation
www.epilepsyfoundation.org

Lupus Foundation of America
www.lupus.org

National Organization for Rare Diseases
www.rarediseases.org

Disclaimer

The websites listed on this page were active at the time of publication. The publisher is not responsible for websites that have changed their address or discontinued operation since the date of publication. The publisher will review and update the websites upon each reprint.

Index

About the Authors

Zachary Chastain is an independent writer and actor living in Binghamton, NY. He is the author of various educational books for both younger and older audiences.

Camden Flath is a writer living and working in Binghamton, New York. He has a degree in English and has written several books for young people. He is interested in current political, social, and economic issues and applies those interests to his writing.

About the Consultant

Dr. Carolyn Bridgemohan is board certified in developmental behavioral pediatrics and practices at the Developmental Medicine Center at Children's Hospital Boston. She is the director of the Autism Care Program and an assistant professor at Harvard Medical School. Her specialty areas are autism and other pervasive developmental disorders, developmental and learning problems, and developmental and behavioral pediatrics.